Greater Than a Tourist Book Series Revi

I think the series is wonderful and beneficial for tourists to get information before visiting the city.
-Seckin Zumbul, Izmir Turkey

I am a world traveler who has read many trip guides but this one really made a difference for me. I would call it a heartfelt creation of a local guide expert instead of just a guide.
-Susy, Isla Holbox, Mexico

New to the area like me, this is a must have!
-Joe, Bloomington, USA

This is a good series that gets down to it when looking for things to do at your destination without having to read a novel for just a few ideas.
-Rachel, Monterey, USA

Good information to have to plan my trip to this destination.
-Pennie Farrell, Mexico

Aptly titled, you won't just be a tourist after reading this book. You'll be greater than a tourist!
-Alan Warner, Grand Rapids, USA

Thank you for a fantastic book.
-Don, Philadelphia, USA

Tina Thanabalan

Great ideas for a port day.

-Mary Martin USA

Even though I only have three days to spend in San Miguel in an upcoming visit, I will use the author's suggestions to guide some of my time there. An easy read - with chapters named to guide me in directions I want to go.

-Robert Catapano, USA

Great insights from a local perspective! Useful information and a very good value!

-Sarah, USA

This series provides an in-depth experience through the eyes of a local. Reading these series will help you to travel the city in with confidence and it'll make your journey a unique one.

-Andrew Teoh, Ipoh, Malaysia

Tourists can get an amazing "insider scoop" about a lot of places from all over the world. While reading, you can feel how much love the writer put in it.

-Vanja Živković, Sremski Karlovci, Serbia

>TOURIST

GREATER THAN A TOURIST – PENANG MALAYSIA

50 Travel Tips from a Local

Tina Thanabalan

Tina Thanabalan

Greater Than a Tourist- Penang Malaysia Copyright © 2018 by CZYK Publishing LLC. All Rights Reserved.

All rights reserved. No part of this book may be reproduced in any form or by any electronic or mechanical means including information storage and retrieval systems, without permission in writing from the author. The only exception is by a reviewer, who may quote short excerpts in a review.

Cover designed by Ivana Stamenković
Cover images: https://pixabay.com/en/penang-malaysia-national-park-2415478/

Greater Than a Tourist
Visit our website at www.GreaterThanaTourist.com

Lock Haven, PA
All rights reserved.

ISBN: 9781980552208

>TOURIST

50 TRAVEL TIPS FROM A LOCAL

Tina Thanabalan

BOOK DESCRIPTION

Are you excited about planning your next trip?
Do you want to try something new?
Would you like some guidance from a local?

If you answered yes to any of these questions, then this Greater Than a Tourist book is for you.

Greater Than a Tourist- Penang Malaysia by Tina Thanabalan offers the inside scoop on Penang. Most travel books tell you how to travel like a tourist. Although there is nothing wrong with that, as part of the Greater Than a Tourist series, this book will give you travel tips from someone who has lived at your next travel destination.

In these pages, you will discover advice that will help you throughout your stay. This book will not tell you exact addresses or store hours but instead will give you excitement and knowledge from a local that you may not find in other smaller print travel books.

Travel like a local. Slow down, stay in one place, and get to know the people and the culture. By the time you finish this book, you will be eager and prepared to travel to your next destination.

Tina Thanabalan

TABLE OF CONTENTS

BOOK DESCRIPTION vii
TABLE OF CONTENTS ix
DEDICATION 1
ABOUT THE AUTHOR 3
HOW TO USE THIS BOOK 5
FROM THE PUBLISHER 7
OUR STORY 9
WELCOME TO 11
> TOURIST 11
INTRODUCTION 13
Things to do in Penang: Heritage 15
1. Bangkok Lane's striking architecture 15
2. Get a religious tour 15
3. Go through Georgetown's heritage streets 16
4. Finding a place to stay 17
Hostels 17
Hotels 18
Beach hotels 18
5. Trishaw tour of Georgetown 18
6. Back in time at Clan Jetties 19
7. Go back in artisanal history 19
8. Local souvenirs 20
9. Chinese clan house 20
10. Stock up on nutmeg 20
11. Penang hill 21
12. Beaches of Batu Ferringhi 22

13. Waterfalls...23
14. Short sea voyage by ferry 24
15. Learn to cook authentic Penang cuisine 24
16. ESCAPE theme park..25
17. Take the bus...25
18. Rent a bicycle/motorbike 25
19. Go to the temples 26
20. Street Art...27

Things to do in Penang: Food and drink 29
21. Hainan Chicken Rice 29
22. Wantan Mee 30
23. Assam Laksa 30
24. Char Kway Teow 31
25. Nasi Lemak 31
26. Beat the heat with an ice ball 32
27. Nyonya flavors..32
28. Nasi Kandar 33
29. Cendol..33
30. Hainanese style satay 33
31. Chinese pasembur (Cheh hu)...34

Best shopping streets in Penang 35
32. Lorong Kulit 35
33. Market Street 35
34. Beach Street 35
35. Campbell Street 36

Best markets in Penang 37
36. Batu Ferringhi Night market..37
37. Little Penang street market 37
38. Macallum Street night market. 38

39. Tanjung Bungah market	38
40. Jalan Kuala Kangsar market	39
41. Malls	39
Where East meets West	40
Things to do in Penang: Nightlife	40
42. Love Lane & Chulia Street	41
43. Reggae Club	41
44. Coffee Tea or Me	41
46. Party Hostels	42
47. Pool tables and Darts	43
48. Rooftop Bars	43
49. Clubs	44
Slippery Senoritas	44
Soju Room	44
George bar	44
Top Reasons	45
to book this trip	45
> TOURIST	47
GREATER THAN A TOURIST	47
> TOURIST	49
GREATER THAN A TOURIST	49
NOTES	50

>TOURIST

DEDICATION

This book is dedicated to the people that I have met on my travels. Especially the people that I can now call my very good friends that I have met in Penang.

Tina Thanabalan

ABOUT THE AUTHOR

Tina Thanabalan is an avid traveler who currently lives in Penang, Malaysia and loves to travel and write about new adventures. Her love of travel comes from a very young age when her parents used to take her places to experience new things. She is originally from Houston, Texas but has roots in Malaysia which is why she chose to settle here for a while.

Tina Thanabalan

HOW TO USE THIS BOOK

The Greater Than a Tourist book series was written by someone who has lived in an area for over three months. The goal of this book is to help travelers either dream or experience different locations by providing opinions from a local. The author has made suggestions based on their own experiences. Please do your own research before traveling to the area in case the suggested places are unavailable.

Tina Thanabalan

FROM THE PUBLISHER

Traveling can be one of the most important parts of a person's life. The anticipation and memories that you have are some of the best. As a publisher of the Greater Than a Tourist book series, as well as the popular 50 Things to Know book series, we strive to help you learn about new places, spark your imagination, and inspire you. Wherever you are and whatever you do I wish you safe, fun, and inspiring travel.

Lisa Rusczyk Ed. D.
CZYK Publishing

Tina Thanabalan

OUR STORY

Traveling is a passion of the "Greater than a Tourist" series creator. Lisa studied abroad in college, and for their honeymoon Lisa and her husband toured Europe. During her travels to Malta, an older man tried to give her some advice based on his own experience living on the island since he was a young boy. She was not sure if she should talk to the stranger but was interested in his advice. When traveling to some places she was wary to talk to locals because she was afraid that they weren't being genuine. Through her travels, Lisa learned how much locals had to share with tourists. Lisa created the "Greater Than a Tourist" book series to help connect people with locals. A topic that locals are very passionate about sharing.

Tina Thanabalan

>TOURIST

WELCOME TO
> TOURIST

Tina Thanabalan

INTRODUCTION

"For my part, I travel not to go anywhere, but to go. I travel for travel's sake. The great affair is to move."

– Robert Louis Stevenson

When it comes to going on a trip, the most stressful part for most people is the planning process. Where to go, what to see, what to eat, etc. However, the common thing that people are interested in is not just the common tourist things that you can find on any old vacation website. They want the ability to get a local idea of a place. So the question is are you ready for your next trip?

Greater Than a Tourist – Penang, Malaysia by Tina Thanabalan gives a better idea of what to do in Penang without the hassle and confusion and will allow you to combine seeing the tourist sites and get a better idea with travel tips from some who lives at your travel destination.

You will be able to get some local advice that will make you feel like a local in no time. The key to loving a place is understanding the people and the culture and truly immersing and embracing your surroundings.

If someone were to ask me about a country that is multi-cultural and multi-ethnic, the first that comes to mind would be Malaysia. Even though Malaysia is predominantly ethnically Malay, there is also a large majority of Malaysian Chinese and Malaysian Indians. It became part of the Straits Settlements from the British, but before it was established by Malay kingdoms. However, because it was part of the Straits Settlement, there are still influences all around the country from the British and the other countries that came to Malaysia; including the Portuguese and the Dutch.

Penang is a very good example of British influence in Malaysia. It is considered to be the most populous island city in Malaysia and because of its magnificent buildings, its capital, Georgetown has been inducted as a UNESCO World Heritage Site in 2008. The history of Penang is very interesting because it was the first British possessions in Southeast Asia.

Just walking around the city you realize and can breathe in the history and culture of the place.

>TOURIST

Things to do in Penang: Heritage

1. Bangkok Lane's striking architecture

Bangkok Lane is special because of its history. It reflects the Thai and Burmese communities of Penang. It is lined with houses that were built by a prominent family in Penang in the 1920s and it is remarkably distinct from most of the streets in Penang because it is also a happy marriage between British colonialism and Asian aesthetics.

One thing that you also need to try when you are walking down this street is the Mee Goreng, which is Penang famous and located at Seng Lee Café on the intersection of Lorong Bangkok and Jalan Burma.

2. Get a religious tour

Only in Malaysia can you find all different types of places of worship on one street. It is situated along Jalan Masjid Kapitan Keling and throughout the street you can see Masjid Kapitan Keling, Kuan Yin Temple, St. George's Church, Sri Mahamariamman Temple, Cathedral of Assumption and Khoo Kongsi at each glance.

3. Go through Georgetown's heritage streets

Georgetown is one of the oldest neighborhoods in Penang and it is filled with heritage streets. You will see that there are many refurbished shop lots that have now become contemporary cafes, boutique hotels, and dive bars. There are also still shop lots that still remain as antique stores, traditional workshops, and Chinese coffee shops.

The history of Penang is a very interesting one, the modern history of Penang only started in 1786 because Captain Francis Light of the British East India Company landed on Penang Island which is where Fort Cornwallis now stands. For Light, Penang was the ideal places because it was in the middle of the maritime trade routes between China and India so it was convenient place for trade and it was a great place for French and Dutch expansion in Southeast Asia. The British influence is so high here that the street names in Penang have English names for example; the city itself is called Georgetown. There are streets here like Lorong Buckingham, Armenian Street, Leith Street, etc.

4. Finding a place to stay.

Finding a place to stay in Penang is so easy. I mean with the internet you just need to google it, but if you are one of those people who just like to show up in a place and find accommodation, you can do that too. There is an influx of places to stay around Penang. However, my advice would be to stay in Georgetown because that is where everything is.

Hostels

If you are a budget traveler, hostels are definitely what you are looking for. They are scattered all over Georgetown and obviously varies in price. But, the common range is between 20-40 RM. One of the cool things about hostels in Georgetown is that they used old buildings and they refurbish it so that it looks and becomes a hostel.

Some hostels that I recommend are; Siok Hostel, which is a bit of a distance from Love Lane, but it is still walking distance. Old Penang Guesthouse, which is located right on Love Lane and is built in an old heritage home so it has its charm with the old tiles and wooden floors and staircase. I also recommend Red Inn Heritage or any of the Red Inn hostels because the beds are super comfy and the staff are so friendly. They are scattered all throughout Georgetown but one is located right on Love Lane and the other is located in Little India. Finally, if you are up for a party, the hostel that you need to be at is Tipsy Tiger Party Hostel. It is definitely the epitome of a party hostel and you get great deals on drinks when you stay there, but you can also party there if you are staying at other hostels.

Hotels

You can experience the best of old and new by staying at any refurbished heritage building. There are so many types of boutique hotels around Penang and Georgetown depending on your price range. I don't have much experience in hotels because I am a budget traveler who has been living in hostels since I have been here. But, one hotel that I can truly recommend is Muntri Grove Hotel located on Muntri Street, just off of Love Lane. It is absolutely beautiful and something that needs to be seen.

Beach hotels

Batu Ferrighi is famous for its beaches and because of that, it is where all the beach resorts are located. They are obviously a bit on the pricey side and about a 30 minute drive from Georgetown.

5. Trishaw tour of Georgetown

Scattered around the city are trishaw guides situated at any main intersection. It is very relaxing if you want someone to cycle you around the town. You can see various sights within an hour or more depending on how long you book the trishaw for. You can negotiate with the driver, but usually the average price is around RM30 per hour.

6. Back in time at Clan Jetties

Something to definitely see in Georgetown because they are unique Chinese settlements that have been around since around the 19th century. It is actually a village on stilts that used to house Chinese immigrants and now their families live there. There are around 8 different clans that still live at the jetties and each jetty is named after the families' surname. To this day, there are still families that live there so if you want to take photos, ask permission first.

7. Go back in artisanal history

Penang is considered to one of the places where you can find traditional artisanal artists. One of the types of crafts that seem to be dying is rattan weaving. When you step in Thean Seng Huat, it is almost like you are stepping back in time because the building itself does not show any sign of being refurbished. However, Ng Poh Yong founded this shop of rattan weaving in the 1930s and it continues with his son who can weaves any type of craft at ease. Get something from them or just watch them master their craft.

8. Local souvenirs

There are so many things that you can take back from Penang. However, this specific place used to be a goldsmith business that has been converted into a local souvenir store that preserves the 1950s and 60s. It is also really cool because at the back in the courtyard, there is still the old equipment dated back to the goldsmith times.

9. Chinese clan house

Back in the day, Kongsis or clan houses were large compounds that housed numerous living areas for multiple families that belong to the same Chinese clan. Each kongsi consists of an administrative building with meeting halls and offices, an opera stage, with multiple terrace houses and shophouses Where are multiple kongsis around but the most famous ones are the Blue Mansion located on Lebuh Leith and Khoo Kongsi located on Lebuh Cannon.

10. Stock up on nutmeg

Penang Is known for its different variation of nutmeg and the best place to find that is at Chowrasta Bazaar. This place is somewhere if you want to see how the locals live, it is where they purchase their daily groceries and it is dominated with vendors selling sweets, pickled fruits and local fried chips. There is also a wet market at the back where people can by fresh meat, vegetables, and fish.

There is also an indoor market where you can find a great selection of second hand books that you can get books for just 3 RM each! It is open from 8:30am-8pm located on Jalan Penang.

Things to do in Penang: Attractions and activities

11. Penang hill

Penang Hill was one of the first colonial hill station developed in Peninsular Malaysia. It was discovered soon after British settlement when Francis Light commissioned the area to be cleared to grow strawberries. On a clear day, you can see the mountains of Langkawi on a clear day. However, during the night time, the sight of a lit-up Georgetown is pretty great as well. The hike is pretty great for most people because they can enjoy the cool, unpolluted air with multiple nature trails. There are also about 100 species of birdlife, ranging from ordinary garden species to exotic deep forest inhabitants. There is also a 220m walkway that is suspended between towering trees 30m about dense jungle that offers great views of the hillside.

There is also the Penang Hill Railway which is the most popular way to get to the top of the hill. It is located at the foot of the hill and it is one of the world's oldest train system and has a 2,007m-long track that takes about 30 minutes to get to the top. As much as it is a relatively long trip, it takes you through wonderful greenery and bungalows that were originally built for British officials and other wealthy citizens.

Another way up to the top is by a 5 km drive up a private road that is only accessible to vehicles of hillside residents. However, if you pay a certain fee you can also take the road. There is also a well-marked 8 km path that leads up from Moon Gate at the Botanical Gardens, it takes about 1 hour but it is a nice walk with plenty of places to rest along the way.

12. Beaches of Batu Ferringhi

The national park consists of both land and sea and it is used by scientists, researchers, and nature lovers to explore its natural treasures.

It was previously known as Pantai Acheh Forest Reserve and it is home to about 417 different kinds of flora and 143 different fauna species. It is located at the northwestern tip of Penang island and was declared a national park in April 2003. The national park is the first protected area under the Malaysia's National Park Act of 1980 and was established to preserve and protect flora and fauna.

There are two beaches in the national park; Monkey beach and Turtle beach. There are two ways to get to both beaches. You can either hike for about an hour and a half to get the Monkey beach and while that is the scenic route, it is a long hike. The other way to get there is by taking a boat and depending on the boat driver, one way can range from around 50RM-70RM. Word of advice is to try and find a group of people to join the expense together.

These are just a few nature things you can do while in Penang, there are many nature trails as well if you are an avid hiker. But all in all, Penang is one of those place where you can enjoy the best of both worlds; nature and city life.

13. Waterfalls

When it comes to nature, one of the most beautiful things to see are the waterfalls and Penang has quite a few of those. The most popular waterfall open to the public is the Titi Kerawang falls near Pantai Acheh. It is located on the west coast of the island on a mountain road that connects the small town of Balik Pulau with the fishing village of Teluk Bahang. It is about 100 meters from the main road and there is a path that leads you there.

Another waterfall in Penang is the Bayan Lepas Waterfall which is located just outside the town of Bayan Lepas. The area around the waterfall has been developed and beautified by the local waterway department. A bridge has been built across the cascades and the waterbank has been paved so that vehicles can enter and exit. There is also a wooden pavilion where you can have a picnic while you enjoy the scenery of the waterfall. The waterfall itself has a height of just about 5 meters and it flows down smooth rocks into a pool where swimming is possible.

Finally, the biggest waterfall is Penang is the Botanical Gardens waterfall. It is within the Penang waterworks department so it remains a restricted area where access is controlled. It used to be one of the most famous waterfalls in Malaysia. However, now because of the waterworks department, you need to seek approval from the authorities to go to this waterfall. It was established in 1910 and it is definitely a sight that people should try and see.

14. Short sea voyage by ferry

There are many ways to get onto the island but a nice relaxing way is to get a ferry from mainland Penang so you can enjoy a fresh sea breeze while enjoying the slow trip to the island. If you are traveling by vehicle, you can just drive up a ramp and park on the ferry itself. The public transportation system in Langkawi is connected to each other so you can always get the bus or taxi from the ferry station.

15. Learn to cook authentic Penang cuisine

The best way to know about any cuisine is to learn how to cook it. The best places here to learn to do that are Tropical Spice Garden and Nazlina Spice Station. Both of these classes are fun and the teachers definitely make it very satisfying. Before every class, Nazlina always begins her classes with a tour of the wet market in Georgetown and you will always end up eating what you are cooking and taking back a skill for when you get home.

>TOURIST

16. ESCAPE theme park

If you are a big fan of theme parks, it would be a good idea to take some time off of the craziness of Georgetown and go to ESCAPE theme park. Located in Jalan Teluk Bahang, it is surrounded by large trees and lush greenery and it is right next to the Butterfly Park. There are over 20 rides and attractions for people to enjoy and you can spend the whole day there.

17. Take the bus

The amazing thing about Penang is the amazing access to public transportation. One of the best ways to get around is through the bus. The Rapid Penang bus is one of the easiest and cheapest ways to get around the island. It goes throughout the island and there are parts that go through the old part of Georgetown before hitting the expressway so it is a good way to watch the landscape change from a concrete jungle to lush greenery.

18. Rent a bicycle/motorbike

Sometimes the best way to explore a new place is just using your own two legs. However, in Penang there are so many ways that you can explore this great place. You can rent a bicycle or motorbike for a day and take it around the whole island for a very cheap price. There are so many shops that let you rent them all you have to do is ask and they will give you the right bike so that it won't hurt your bum at the end of the day. If you want to rent a bicycle, it is about 15 RINGGIT for 24 hours and for motorbikes, it is about 35 RINGGIT for 24 hours with a 150RM deposit. However, you need to make sure that you have international driver's license or if you are from the UK your regular license should be ok.

A high percentage of bikes that are used and rented out in Penang can also be used as mountain bikes which means that you are use them to go offroading around the wilderness of Penang. There are also several routes that you can take to explore the island. If you are up for an adventure, the most common route is from Georgetown and head south to Bayan Lepas then to Balik Lulau, Teluk Bahang, Batu Ferrighi and heading back to Georgetown through Tanjung Bungah and Tanjung Tokong. The route itself is about 82 km long and takes an experienced cyclist about 6 hours to complete if you are up for the challenge.

19. Go to the temples

Kek Lok Si temple is considered to be the largest and best known Chinese temple in Penang. In Hokkien it is referred to as the "Temple of Supreme Bliss" It overlooks the Air Itam Village in the central part of the island. The best way to get there is either by Grab or by bus. The hillside, which is named Crane Mountain, is considered to be a good location and retreat for Taoists practitioners that are striving for immortality. It combines Mahayana Buddhism with Taoist beliefs and other Chinese rituals and beliefs. The construction of the temple began in 1890 and was completed in 1905. It was inspired by Beow Lean, the chief monk of the Goddess of Mercy temple at Pitt street

If you are deathly afraid of snakes like I am this next temple is not the best place for you. The Snake Temple in Bayan Lepas is considered to be the only temple of its kind in the world. It is filled with the smoke of burning incense but not only that but a variety of pit vipers. It is believed that they are harmless because of the smoke but as a precaution the snakes have been de-venomed but with their fangs still intact. The temple was built around the 1850s in memory of Chor Soo Kong by a Buddhist monk. According to legend, he was very serious about seeking spiritual attainment and was ordained by the temple at a very young age. The reason why snakes were added to the temple is because it was said that he would sometimes give shelter to the snakes of the jungle.

20. Street Art

Since Penang has been around for so long, the buildings date back to the 1700s which means a lot of them are rundown, but people have tried to renovate and make them look stunning. Artists and muralists alike have tried to enhance Georgetown's position as the street capital of the country. Since 2008, Georgetown was inscribed as a World Heritage Site and because of that the street art has developed at a very rapid rate. In 2009, cartoonists such as Tang Mun Kian and Baba Chuah wanted to help bring awareness to the history of the street by adding the stories of street and social history through the use of caricatures so there are metal caricatures that have been set up all over

Tina Thanabalan

the city for everyone to see. The iron caricatures blend humor and historical facts that describe and colloquial demeanor of early settlement days that gave a memorable history to each of those streets. They depict the daily lives of the people where those landmarks start at this moment.

In 2012, London-trained Lithuanian artist Ernest Zacharevic was asked and commissioned to paint a collection of murals around the inner city and you can see them all over Georgetown. The project sparks interest with the locals and more and more local artists are starting to add murals to the walls of Georgetown.

Now, rather than walking around aimlessly, most hostels and hotels will have a brochure of all the street art so that you can go on a scavenger hunt around the town so that you can take photos of all of the murals and sculptures. Being interested in street art myself, I was excited to start my tour so with a coffee and my brochure in hand, I was ready for my adventure around Georgetown to see all the street art.

>TOURIST

Things to do in Penang: Food and drink

Penang is considered to be a diverse city filled with locals, expats, and travelers alike. Because of that, there are so many different types of cuisine in Penang. It is probably one of the most famous places for the ample amounts of street food. However, for people that are not used to eating on plastic chairs and on the side of the road the concept may seem daunting. However, street food is the way of life for most Malaysians because its inexpensive and easy. It is possible that there may even be restaurants that move around and they are not in the same place ever so it is necessary to try those places because they are the most popular. Because of the mix of cultures, it is also possible to find restaurants and hotels all over but you don't really get to know the culture of the place do you?

21. Hainan Chicken Rice

One of my personal favorites is Hainan Chicken Rice. It is a dish that has been adapted from early Chinese immigrants from Southern China. The chicken itself is prepared by poaching the chicken in boiling temperature and the stock is skimmed off and the chicken is roasted or steamed with garlic, ginger, pandan leaves, and other seasonings to produce a delicious treat. One of my favorite places to get Chicken Rice is Goh Thew Chik Hainan Chicken Rice on Chulia Street. There are so many places to get chicken rice, but this place is pretty amazing. They only serve chicken rice, you ask for anything else they will look at you in a very strange way.

22. Wantan Mee

If there is something that is a must try, it is definitely Wantan Mee from Ah Ngau, he has been selling Wantan Mee at the very same spot for over 30 years and before that his father sold the same noodles. The noodles themselves are homemade from a local noodle maker but that is the only thing that has changed over the past few years, they are flavored with lard, light soya sauce and it is served with minced pork wantans with pickled sliced green chili with sesame oil and pepper. He is also known for his beef noodles which is not something I am even used to. It is from an old Guangzhou recipe and made with beef brisket and rather than it being a clear soup it is a dark broth and is served with the same wantan noodles but they have a very distinct taste.

23. Assam Laksa

Something that seems to be an acquired taste. Assam Laksa is a very famous Penang dish and it is something that most locals swear by. But, for someone who doesn't quite enjoy the taste of anything too fishy it isn't really something for you. The traditional dish is generally a thick broth but the broth is thinner. It is a made with poached mackerel, tamarind, lemongrass, chillies, and shrimp paste. The tamarind makes it have sour undertones and topped with rice vermicelli noodles. However, if Assam Laksa is not the thing for you,

you should definitely try Curry Laksa which is a coconut-based curry soup. In Penang however, it is known as curry mee due to the different noodles that they use. However, the ingredients are the same which includes bean curd puffs, fish sticks, shrimps, cockles, and shredded chicken. Curry mee in Penang uses congealed pork blood which is a delicacy to the Malaysian Chinese community but obviously you don't need to have that at all.

24. Char Kway Teow

Another famous dish in Penang is Penang Char Kway Teow. Traditionally it is made with flat rice noodles and stir fried with dark and light soy sauce with prawns, cockles, bean sprouts, and chopped chives. Every street vendor serves it differently but the concept is still the same. There are some places that serve it on banana leaf so that it absorbs the flavors. While it has a reputation of not being the healthiest dish because of its high saturated fat content, historically it was perfect because it was sold to fishermen, farmers, and cockle-gatherers because of its cheap source of energy and nutrients.

25. Nasi Lemak

One of my favorite dishes is Nasi Lemak. It can be served as breakfast, lunch, or dinner. Translated into English, it is "Fat rice" because its rice is flavored with coconut milk and arranged on a plate with sambal, which is a hot sauce or paste which is made out of a mixture of chili peppers such as shrimp paste, fish sauce, garlic, ginger, shallots, scallion, palm sugar, lime juice, and rice vinegar. It is also added with fried anchovies, peanuts, and hard-boiled eggs. As traditional as the dish is, there are other variations with can include fried chicken or chicken rendang. Which is a dish that involves meat pieces that are slowly cooked in coconut milk and spices until almost all the liquid is gone and allowing the meat to become tender and absorb the condiments.

26. Beat the heat with an ice ball

Ice balls are a type of nostalgic remembrance for all local Malaysians. It is basically just a shaved ice ball and each sphere is handmade by tightly packing shaved ice into a ball and drenching it with syrup of your choice. My favorite is a combination of lychee, mango, and kiwi. It is something to enjoy on a very hot day. It can be a messy and sticky process but it makes you feel like a kid again.

27. Nyonya flavors.

Nyonya cuisine is something that you can only find in Malaysia. It is also called Peranakan Chinese or Straits-born Chinese and it is the combination of Malay and Chinese cuisine. The flavors are intense, but something that needs to be tried. It is most commonly found in Malacca, but can also be found in different parts of Malaysia including Penang.

28. Nasi Kandar

Nasi Kandar is something very common of locals because of the prices. Basically every restaurant will give you a heaping pile of rice and you can choose from a variation of dishes that range from vegetarian to meat dishes and also ranges in spice level. Depending on what you get, you are almost likely only going to spend around 10RM for a meal.

29. Cendol

There are so many different desserts in Malaysia, but the one that stands out is cendol. It is a sweet Indian/Malay dessert that has the right combination of ingredients and it is served ice cold. It is made out of finely shaved ice, red beans, aromatic palm sugar syrup, rich coconut milk, and soft green rice flour noodles that are made from mixing rice flour and the juice of fragrant pandan leaves. You can either get it plain or you can add sticky rice to it. It is the best thing for a hot day.

30. Hainanese style satay

This street food is very popular for locals and tourists alike. It is all about the preparation that intrigues people. It is made over charcoals so that it has that charcoal flavor with a few burnt bits. You can get either chicken or pork but there are some places that also serve beef.

They are normally served in skewer form and you will normally find two pieces of cut lean pork with a piece of pork fat in between. The marinade for the satay normally is turmeric, salt, and pepper. It is grilled over charcoal and brushed with a basting sauce that is made out of coconut milk and oil and using a stalk of lemongrass. It is normally served with fresh cucumbers, onions, and peanut sauce.

31. Chinese pasembur (Cheh hu)

In Hokkien, the direct translation mean raw fish, which is strange because there is no raw fish in it at all. It is usually made with shredded strips of cucumber, Chinese yam bean, bean cake, light and puffy flour fritters, and crispy prawn crackers. The whole thing is tossed in a potato gravy and garnished with roasted sesame seeds which results in a wonderful mixture of textures and flavors.

>TOURIST

Best shopping streets in Penang

32. Lorong Kulit

In English, it means Skin lane in reference to its history as a leather/tannery area. It has so been known as "Thieves market" it is where you can find second hand goods. You should definitely go into it with the concept of "one person's trash is another person's treasure" You can basically find anything vintage. If you are aware of Chatuchak market in Bangkok, it is very similar in which you are find absolutely everything.

33. Market Street

This is the main street in Little India and you can find everything from jewelry, traditional Indian outfits to wholesale spices. Just taking a walk from Little India you can find an insane amount of restaurants that are vegetarian or non-vegetarian.

34. Beach Street

Historically, this used to be a trading street and it takes you back in time and shows people goods that used to be traded through Penang and it introduces people to traditional tradesmen. You can find teas at a certain store, you can even find Arabic delights at Souq Al-Arabia and you can find one of the oldest spice traders in Penang. If you are interested in sewing or jewelry making you can also find that there.

35. Campbell Street

You can find practically the same things of Campbell street as you can on Beach street, so it really depends on your location and where you want to go and what you want to find. There are jewelers, handicraftsmen, tea sellers, etc.

Best markets in Penang

Asia is one of those places where shopping can ranges between super cheap because of the markets and expensive because of the malls. There are multiple night markets in Penang, most in Georgetown but some are scattered across the island. Traditionally called a "pasar malam" vendors usually sell things from snack foods to clothing because depending on where it is and what day of the week, some can be quite large.

36. Batu Ferringhi Night market

This night market is about 1 km long and it provides shoppers with more than 100 stalls where you can buy anything from batik prints to sporting goods. There are also some vendors that sell homeware items like decorative plates and embroidered pillow cases and you can even find handcrafted bejeweled accessories. It is open from 6:00pm daily and you can even find pop stores from different artists and designers.

37. Little Penang street market

This market is a monthly bazaar that takes place on Upper Penang Road every last Sunday of the month from 10:00-5:00. It Is a nonprofit community venture that is operated voluntarily by locals. It is a lively and diverse market that can be described as culturally hip because it frequented by the young and urban crowd. The focus of the market is to support small and local businesses and artists and they usually sell personally-sourced antiques, homemade jewelry, etc. There are also designated spots for hourly book readings and traditional music and dance performances.

38. Macallum Street night market.

It only operates on Monday nights from 7:00-11:00 and it offers some of the cheapest finds on the island. It is like every other market, but they pride themselves on being the cheapest on the island. The only problem with that is that the quality can be questionable. There are obviously also street vendors that sell food that they definitely do not disappoint. It is located on Lintang Macallum 1, Pengkalan Weld in Georgetown.

39. Tanjung Bungah market

It is a wet market located in Tanjung Tokong and it very local. You can tell that there are definitely regulars that go there to buy their fresh produce. It is a great way to see how the locals live. Not only does it have fresh produce, but it also sells prepacked foods that you can buy once you have wandered the market if you are a bit pekish. On Tuesday nights, the market opens for longer and transforms into a night market with even more stalls.

40. Jalan Kuala Kangsar market

It is located very close to the Chowrasta bazaar and it is a morning market where you can also find fresh produce. If you are looking for places to have breakfast, there are also Chinese coffee shops along that area so you can stop in for a coffee and some traditional Chinese breakfast.

41. Malls

There are obviously also malls in Georgetown which includes Prangin Mall and First Avenue where they sell electronics and there are also hairdressers and they sell things for relatively cheap as well. They also have the common stores like H&M and such. If you travel a bit further, you can also go to Gurney Plaza or Gurney Paragon which is where most of the expats go if they want to go grocery shopping.

Tina Thanabalan

Where East meets West

Because of the influx of expats and travelers, there have been an abundance of Western restaurants and cafes all over town. Georgetown is one of those places that has influences from all over the place. If you are like me and enjoy sitting at a coffee shop all day working on your laptop there are a few places that you can definitely do that.

One of my favorite places to hang out is Wheeler's. It is a small quaint little place on Love Lane where there are always regulars and newcomers that become family. You can always just sit here and get some food or coffee and just hang out here with your laptop. Another place to hang out is Mugshot Café where they do incredible bagels and coffee, it is also connected to a bakery if you like just a simple croissant or want some bread for your morning breakfast.

There are so many different cafés and coffee shops that are scattered around the city, all you have to do is look for them. Each have their own vibe and are very enjoyable.

Things to do in Penang: Nightlife

With every city comes great nightlife and Penang does not disappoint. Whether you are a local or a traveller, you will find a great place to have a few drinks or dance the night away. It has everything from different price ranges if you are on a budget. No matter your music, DJ, or cocktail preference you will be able to find whatever you want in Penang.

42. Love Lane & Chulia Street

Normally, my go-to place for a night out would be Love Lane. During the day, it is a family friendly environment with coffee shops and restaurants, but at night the adults come out to play. It is one of the most famous streets for a night out in Georgetown. Most bars on this street give happy hour prices all night long and you realize that your money can go a long way.

43. Reggae Club

One of my favorite bars to drink at would be Reggae Club on Chulia Street, which is the road perpendicular to Love Lane. If you are a lady well you are in luck. They do ladies hour where you can get mixers for free from 6pm-9pm. They also have live music every day and if you are a musician it is the perfect place to jam. Hopefully, you aren't scared of dogs because they are two tiny dogs that hang out there all the time.

44. Coffee Tea or Me

Speaking of dogs, I am pretty sure that everyone has heard of a dog or cat café but have you heard of a husky bar? Well, Georgetown has its very own husky bar. The main attraction at Coffee Tea or Me bar are the three huskies that just chill in the bar. They also have really great promotions and awesome games that you can play with friends or strangers that will slowly become friends.

45. Holy Guacamole

Another awesome bar that you should check out is Holy Guacamole. The second you walk in, you can see the theme is very true to the Mexican way of life with the tiles and the Dia de Los Muertos Calaveras on the wall. The food is also pretty authentic but the best part is the happy hour prices. 10 RM for a margarita! But, not just margaritas. There are also happy hour prices for mojitos, beer, and daiquiris. They also have live music most night and they play everything and anything.

46. Party Hostels

I have to say that I have never been the biggest fan of staying at party hostel, however, one thing that I have to admit is that it they are definitely a fun night out. One of the best party hostel that I have ever partied at is Tipsy Tiger Hostel. You walk in and you get a total party hostel vibe and every day of the week has different promotions for in-house guests and outside guests as well. On Wednesdays, they have ladies night where women get free drinks from 8pm-10pm and if guys dress up at women and put makeup on, they also get free drinks.

47. Pool tables and Darts

Now, if you are one of those people who enjoy playing pool, darts, or any activity at a bar the two places you should definitely check out are Fidalgo and Soho Freehouse. Fidalgo is located right on Chulia street and is very hard to miss as it is a giant blue building. When you head upstairs you will see an array of dartboards that you can play while you have your drinks. Another great place to have a few drinks and play some games is Soho Freehouse. It is away from the main strip but it is nice to see a local bar. There are pool tables set up so you can enjoy a beer and play some pool.

48. Rooftop Bars

If you like a have a view of the city, one of the best places to go to is ThreeSixty Revolving Restaurant and Skybar. It sits on top of Bayview Hotel and you can see the wonderful views of Penang island's city center. There is a two-level penthouse lounge and the indoor level is home to a dining room that does a slow 360-degree turn. There is also a open-air lounge when you can sit in armchairs and truly enjoy the view.

Another rooftop bar that you can enjoy is The Press Rooftop Bar. Located along Chulia Street, it is a posh two-storey nightclub where downstairs is a small, intimate space done up with lots of golden dark wood with a mix of techno, R&B, hip hop and soul. While the rooftop, is an open air-space that have a mix of seating arrangements and they also have chairs that are closer to the edge so you can get a great view.

Tina Thanabalan

49. Clubs

Slippery Senoritas

One club that always seems to come up when I talk to locals is Slippery Senoritas. Opened in 2001, it brings in a vibrant crowd because of its two floors for dancing and drinking; the main dance floor gives the feel of a South American dance club. It coins itself as "more than a dance club" because it has 'flair' bartenders who perform every night with bottle-juggling and fire-breathing performances.

Soju Room

Another club that seems to be pretty famous in Georgetown is Soju Room. It is located at the basement of Penang Time Square and it is one of the oldest dance clubs in Penang. It is usually popular amongst local Penangites and it is decorated in a simple black and white style but lit up by neon laser lights and a big dance floor. They have an eclectic music soundtrack with almost every genre that can include classic rock, indie electro, metal and even punk and grunge.

George bar

Finally, one of my favorite clubs in Georgetown is George Bar. During the day, the front of house is a pizza joint that also serves alcohol and you can get All You Can Drink for 60 RM. However, at around 12:30, the back of house opens and it is a club. They take the George theme to an interesting level and the décor inside is very

>TOURIST

simple but it is still a great night out. Drinks are pretty inexpensive for a club and it is located right on Love Lane.

Top Reasons to book this trip

1) **The culture**: There is so much culture in Penang that everywhere you walk, there is something to learn about the city and the country as a whole.

2) **The food**: The food is a combination of everything and it will definitely not disappoint

3) **The mix**: Penang is one of those places where you can be in the middle of a city with apartments everywhere, you can be surrounded by historical places, and also be on a beach.

One of the most ideal places for everything and one of my favorite places that I have ever lived.

Tina Thanabalan

> TOURIST
GREATER THAN A TOURIST

Visit GreaterThanATourist.com:
http://GreaterThanATourist.com

Sign up for the Greater Than a Tourist Newsletter:
http://eepurl.com/cxspyf

Follow us on Facebook:
https://www.facebook.com/GreaterThanATourist

Follow us on Pinterest:
http://pinterest.com/GreaterThanATourist

Follow us on Instagram:
http://Instagram.com/GreaterThanATourist

Follow on Twitter:
http://twitter.com/ThanaTourist

Tina Thanabalan

> TOURIST
GREATER THAN A TOURIST

Please leave your honest review of this book on Amazon and Goodreads. Thank you. We appreciate your positive and constructive feedback. Thank you.

Tina Thanabalan

NOTES

Milton Keynes UK
Ingram Content Group UK Ltd.
UKHW041312161223
434508UK00004B/324